Existence Shining As Awareness

Existence Shining As Awareness: Commentaries *on* Ramana Maharshi's *Sat Darshanam*

ISBN-13: 978-1-7367044-0-0

Cover and book design by Robert Grey.

Existence Shining As Awareness

COMMENTARIES *on* RAMANA MAHARSHI'S
SAT DARSHANAM
by
James Swartz

SHINING WORLD

ShiningWorld.com

By James Swartz:

Existence Shining As Awareness: Commentaries on Ramana Maharshi's Sat Darshanam

The Fire of Self-Knowledge: Commentaries on Shankaracharya's Atma Bodha

Mandukya Upanishad and Gaudapada's Karika

The Yoga of the Three Energies

The Yoga of Love

The Book of Charts: A Visual Road Map to Enlightenment

Meditation: Inquiry into the Self

Inquiry into Existence: The Lamp of Knowledge

The Mystery of the Trinity: Love and Knowledge

The Essence of Enlightenment: Vedanta, the Science of Consciousness

How to Attain Enlightenment: The Vision of Non-Duality

Experience and Knowledge

Mystic by Default

CONTENTS

Preface 1

I **The Topics** 2
   The I Experience, Not *the* Experience *of the* I 2
   No Thinking, Traditional Thinking, Wrong Thinking 2
   Absorbed *in the* Vision *of* Non-Duality 3
   The Teaching 5
   Existence/Awareness/Bliss 7
   Accumulation 9
   Duality: *the* Subject-Object Split 10
   Devotion 10
   See *the* Is-ness, Not *the* Thought-ness 13
   The Apparent Reality... 13
   How *to* "See" What Is When What Is Sees?........................ 14
   The Discipline 15

II **Invocation** 16
   Existence Shining As Awareness... 19
      As the mind, so the world. 21
      The light sees the darkness, but the darkness sees not
         the light. 22
   The Living Processes *of* Being 22
   Living Processes.. 24
      The world appears when you wake up. 26
      You can count on knowledge. 26
      Knowledge is true to the object of knowledge. 28
      Drop into the Heart and take a stand in What Is. 29
      Self-knowledge is a loss of ignorance, not a gain of knowledge. ... 29
      Existence is called knowledge when it is associated with a
         thought. 29
      The first person is not the Me. 31
   Accumulation 31
   Karma Yoga and *Jnana Yoga*... 31
   Hedged Love – Attachment.. 32

I don't see. I am Seeing. 34

A Defect *of* Cause *and* Effect 34

See Is Knowing Is Abiding.. 35

    I don't want to see God. 36

    Beautiful, intelligent Ignorance. 37

The Reflection Teaching.. 38

    Shifting your backpack. 39

    The scriptures assert "THAT YOU ARE." 41

    The eye of wisdom sees itself. 42

    I am free when I know and free when I don't know. 44

    Vedanta reveals the unexamined logic of one's own experience. ... 44

Cancel Culture.. 44

Essence *of the* Teaching 46

Preface

THE IDEA THAT liberation is not a discrete experience but is the nature of the Self is probably responsible for the growing interest in Vedanta worldwide. The statement that Self-knowledge is the way to freedom, however, often makes Vedanta unappealing to many modern seekers who dismiss it as only an "intellectual" philosophy. This view is also common among a certain uninformed cult of Ramana fans, who prefer the idea that enlightenment – liberation from a suffering mind – is a one-off experience gained by "grace" that instantly transforms a human being into a spiritual Superbeing. Conveniently, many undisciplined modern people looking for a quick and easy way to transcend the mind endorse the view that rigorous inquiry is not required, although Ramana recommended it and practiced it for twenty years whilst living alone in caves.

To properly set foot on the path of knowledge means that one should not ignore the mind, attempt to transcend or remove it, but to cultivate it assiduously by gradually shifting one's attention from one's person – the "I-sense" – to Being itself, which is seemingly hidden "behind" the mind.

The "I-sense" adds a new term to the idea that humans are cast in the image of God, to use Christian language, or is a reflection of God, to use Vedantic language. As Existence itself, we are always experiencing freedom, whether our "I-sense" appreciates it or not. How the "I-sense" can gain experiential access to its limitless essence is the topic of this brilliant teaching of Ramana Maharshi.

Although I lived behind Ramana's *ashram* for fifteen years, I was not inspired to write commentaries on *Sat Darshanam* until recently when a friend sent me a wonderful transcript of the talks of a modern *mahatma*, Swami Tattvavidananda, a *guru* brother and disciple of the late great Swami Dayananda Saraswati. I have taken the liberty to transform it into a written document that is easily accessible to a sincere inquirer.

This work is dedicated to Ramana Maharshi, whose teachings about the nature of freedom itself have been largely misunderstood by Western seekers who fail to grasp that Ramana does not endorse the view that liberation is a discrete experience of one's innermost Self.

1

I

The Topics

The I Experience, Not the Experience of the I

IF YOU HAVE been studying Vedanta for some time, ask yourself: "Am I the same person today that I was when I began?" If you say yes, you have missed the point, because you don't understand that you are not a person chasing the experience of freedom and non-dual love. You are Existence shining as Consciousness. At the same time, if you are the same person, have there been spontaneous positive changes in your personality? If not, you haven't understood the value of spiritual practice, particularly *karma yoga*, which transforms your mind as it prepares you to accept the fact that you are not a who, you are ever-free, non-dual, Existence shining as Awareness masquerading as a person.

The thinking mentality is a predetermined mold into which you pour your thinking, which only comes out one way. Vedanta says you are wonderful, and indeed you are, but instead of looking to see if it's true here and now, you set out to remove all your objections to this thesis, which takes a long time and may qualify you as a scholar but not necessarily as a simple person who knows the truth. Scholarship that misses the truth of the I only adds another identity to the conceptual person. Instead of becoming simpler, you become more complex and conflicted. Vedanta is a pathless path, and freedom is a living vision.

Yes, just the idea that you are pure and perfect as you are can generate a great awakening culminating in a giddy state of mind and an opinion that you are now particularly wonderful. But it may be that the scriptures are not talking about the same you that you are talking about.

No Thinking, Traditional Thinking, Wrong Thinking

When we are dissatisfied with life and realize that blaming the world doesn't solve the problem, sometimes we start seeking for the answer within. We may hear that thinking itself is the problem and are told to meditate to stop the mind or to "transcend" thinking. But this doesn't work, because the mind is the only useful tool for navigating reality successfully; failure to use it properly results in much suffering.

2

Or we might hear about non-dual thinking. Non-dual thinking is thinking that you are Awareness, which is a good start and often a relief, but putting on a cute little conceptual hat on which the slogan "I am Awareness" is embroidered doesn't work; life goes on as it did before.

"This is not the way to approach Vedanta. Vedanta entails thinking independently from the conceptual binary subject-object split that is based on identification with the physical body." Identifying as the body-mind-sense complex produces inner and outer conflict. Vedanta is not impulsive involuntary thinking, habitual thinking or deliberate thinking. If it can be said to be thinking at all, it is spontaneous thinking based on the actual experience of What Is in every moment. It is thinking based on seeing What Is. Seeing is not thinking; it is experiencing.

Absorbed in the Vision of Non-Duality

Vedanta's vision (*darshan*) is a spontaneous outpouring of a universal inner feeling born of a natural communion with the unborn I, the Is-ness (*sat*). No clever arguments are required to justify it.

There is a source in you deeper than the mind, deeper than your thoughts and emotions. It is a pity to take the mind as your substance, because it isn't you. It is merely an inert collection of material energies. When you say "I feel" as everyone does, you are not talking about an emotion; you are talking about a universal inner experience – Existence experience (*anubhava*). Emotions are only gross positive and negative material energies generated by your fears and desires, dislikes and likes. Existence experience is not a special experience. Every living being is experiencing exactly the same thing always because there is only Existence experience. You say "I am" because you are experiencing Existence. It is the substrate and substance of discrete experiences, including your thoughts and emotions. It is cherished beyond all particular experiences and it is the reason even suffering people want to live another day. More than happiness, it is pure bliss.

If someone asks if you are a man or a woman, you don't say, "Just a minute; I need to feel if I am a man or a woman." In fact men sometimes feel like women, and women sometimes feel like men. *You think you are a man or a woman.* But in reality you are neither a man nor a woman; you are a sentient being first and foremost. Just as our bodies are made of food, all our experiences are made of Existence; there is no other option. We are a universal person.

3

I-you-we exist. We are. Existence is not theoretical or virtual. If you were only allowed to say "I am" when you were asked who you are, the interlocutor would know what you meant because he or she is the same person. The supermarket of identities that is the world offers momentary conceptual identities: father, mother, doctor, lawyer, black, white, rich, poor, Muslim, Christian, American, Chinese, etc. They have nothing to do with What you really are, although they are all born out of the pure original "I-sense" or "I-thought." The "I-sense" does not belong to the Self, because the Self is unborn and non-dual. It doesn't live or die. It is not sentient or insentient. "I-sense" is a living sensation, a feeling that references the self-luminous associationless you, Existence itself. Because of it, we seek freedom. We know that freedom exists because when the mind is uncluttered with desire and fear, we experience intimations of it in our "I-sense."

Since we cannot describe What we are in words, imagination is required. You can call it visualization if you like, but it is not visualizing a new house or car or a soulmate. It is letting your mind flow to the implied meaning of Vedanta's revealing words. For instance, if you speak like a computer without accenting any word in this sentence, "You look good today," it means you look good today. But if you pause a second after the word "good" and emphasize the word "today," it means you didn't look good yesterday.

Imagine a light that was shining before the world began. This light never started shining and will never stop shining. It shines on its own. That immortal light is you, Existence shining as Awareness. Vedanta reveals it. The Sanskrit word for this "light of lights" is *aham anubhuti* (I experience), or as Ramana calls it, *aham spuranam*. You shine, meaning you are aware, but you are not doing one blessed thing to be aware. You were shining when your body appeared and you are shining when it disappears. In pitch darkness, you shine. You shine when your mind bounces light onto the world in the waking state and it shines when your mind is not present in sleep. When you have received this precious teaching, you will confidently proclaim, "I shine and everything shines after me."

The "I-sense" or "I-thought" seemingly arises from the self-shining I – Consciousness/Awareness. This I experience is not a special experience that only famous people like Buddha, Ramana and Shankara are capable of, but is the experience of everyone. These luminaries just knew it.

You can make things with your hands or you can make things with your mind, but you cannot make yourself. The purpose of Vedanta is to reveal the unborn Self shining you, by removing ignorance of it. You are not going to generate Existence experience by any action, spiritual or otherwise. It is present before you even think of doing anything. The thoughts that come from the mind turn into "-isms," ideologies, religions, philosophies and so forth. Vedanta is not an "-ism," an ideology, a system or a philosophy. It is a means of knowing and then forgetting the "I am."

Unfortunately, there is an infinite array of inert worldly and religious thought and feeling objects clustered around the original pure I that distracts it from its innate knowledge of itself, causing it to seemingly forget that it is self-shining bliss. These thought and feeling objects attract us, as they promise some kind of salvation while simultaneously consigning the ever-free but distracted and confused subject to a frustrating zero-sum life.

Giving up objects, activities for instance, is not always easy, but giving up ideas – beliefs and opinions – is often difficult, particularly the products of the mind: political, religious and spiritual ideas, the idea "I know who I am," for instance. We are easily seduced by these ideas and quickly become attached and fixated on them, which as surely as the sun rises and sets daily, unintentionally hides the seeing of the Seer from us.

Your "I-sense" may not agree, but you are not a healthy person if you don't want to see beyond your fixations: security, pleasure, recognition, power and virtue. Just as the moon eclipses the sun, the mind easily hides the Self. The mind needs to step aside and allow you to commune with your essence – the ever-present, ever-free, unborn, self-revealing light – one without a second. To experience the Self that is not an object, you need to work through the distracting thought and feeling objects appearing as discrete experiences, positive and negative, which seem to eclipse it. As long as outer things trouble or fascinate you, you are deprived of the perfect satisfaction of your innate existence. All sensory, emotional and intellectual experiences are subsumed when non-dual vision is awakened. Ramana is speaking from the dimension beyond the mind.

The Teaching

Ramana said he was not a teacher. Did he mean that he was Existence shining as Awareness? Or did he mean that, whereas he was a knower, he was not a teacher in the traditional sense? Or both? We will never know, but it makes no difference, because the essence of the teaching is: Existence shining as Awareness is real and the world of objects is apparently real. When this statement is properly understood, your seeking ends because it ends your identity as a knower and with it the need to claim "I am Awareness."

This knowledge can be assimilated in the traditional format or not. The traditional format is a systematic, word-by-word, verse-by-verse unfolding of the *mantras* of the *Upanishads, Brahma Sutras, Bhagavad Gita* and the commentaries of sages who subjected their minds to the teaching methodology and assimilated the meaning of the essential *mantras*.

The traditional format is excellent but, like all objects in the apparent reality, it is easy to approach with an academic mindset, which in itself is not the spiritual kiss of death, but which tends to stress the importance of accumulated knowledge rather than the immaculate living vision of reality that happens when ignorance is removed and the knowledge that removed it is no longer necessary. Self-knowledge is not a goal. It is a means to an end. The removal of the doer/knower is the goal. Academics are goal-oriented and are tested before a degree is issued by an organization that validates their acquired knowledge.

Vedanta's enlightenment certificate is issued by God. It is the immediate thought-free living vision of reality that validates your true identity as Existence shining as Awareness. You aren't a person. This vision obviates the need for a limited identity. You need to know that your name is Being. Like your worldly name, once you know it, you needn't know it again.

Yes, the "I-sense" has instruments of knowledge, but you aren't the "I-sense." It is an object that appears within the scope of your panoramic multi-dimensional Awareness. The real you cannot know anything, because you do not have instruments of knowledge. If you say you know the Self, you don't know it, because it is not an object that instruments of knowledge can reveal. Knowing it is knowing Being. You simply are. What you are minus thoughts and words is more than enough. Hard and fast Self-knowledge is necessary to destroy seeking, but it too needs to go the way of all things.

Is-ness shining as Awareness only plays the role of a knower when ignorance-generated cognitions are present. It is pure knowing minus cognitions. Knowing is not knowledge. It is Being's dynamic capacity for knowledge that remains untouched by concepts. Vedanta provisionally conceptualizes knowledge and perversely destroys its conceptions at the right time. You can never say "I know" or "I don't know," because you are the Teflon witness of knowledge and ignorance.

You won't say "I know," because you were never ignorant in the first place. Memory, accumulated knowledge, is not involved in Being. When ignorance followed by knowledge goes, you are just a simple ordinary entity free of thoughts yet capable of thinking clearly. Until then remembered knowledge is required.

Existence/Awareness/Bliss

If you are collector of interesting, subtle and profound big-picture ideas, you may love Vedanta. During the sixties an academic was rummaging through the shelves in the City Lights bookstore in San Francisco and happened to knock loose a copy of a spiritual book that a previous customer had carelessly placed on the shelf. He bent down to retrieve the book which had fallen open to a page that said the Self, which he previously imagined to be the guy on his driver's license, was Existence and Awareness and Bliss. He had a revelation. On the basis of this snippet of information he "saw" that Existence created matter, and that Awareness created mind, and that mixing the two together created endless Bliss, knowledge of which he opined was salvation. His ignorance inspired him so much he wrote a big book and started a movement to make the whole world happy, but the world couldn't relate, because his idea wasn't true. He blamed the world and became angry and depressed.

You may be a genius with the best intentions, but you won't figure out what you are on your own on the basis of an epiphany or two. You need an impersonal teaching that ties the seemingly disparate aspects of life into one cogent vision. You need to be to be taught in a systematic manner by someone who has been properly taught. The truth, sad to say, is completely counter-intuitive. Matter, Awareness and Bliss are synonyms. In the right context, they reveal an experiencing witnessing you (*sakshi bhava*) that is unaffected by what it experiences.

You can't intuit, memorize or do your way to freedom and non-dual love. You need the dispassionate enthusiastic mentality of an explorer, a scientist. There is nothing mystical about reality. You are a detective and the case is never solved, even when it is. One verifiable known fact leads to the discovery of another previously known but forgotten fact, on and on until life's colorful kaleidoscopic bits and pieces resolve into one permanent living vision. Because life is fresh every second, you never know what will happen. Around every bend an adventure awaits. Seeing is exciting, energizing and liberating.

Be open and learn. A ninety-year-old professor of linguistics with a to-die-for vocabulary googles every new word he discovers. Is he old? *Darshan*, seeing What Is, is like following links on the internet; you never know where you will be taken. Don't freeze life into a formula so you can quit thinking and rest. Inquiry is a state of mind, a journey without a goal. When you come to a conclusion about something or someone, you slay yourself.

If someone injures you, it does not mean they are a bad person. People are fluid like water, always moving like the wind. The next moment your villain helps an old lady across the street, and you fail to accept what you see, reveals a cynical, perhaps bored, mentality. You may be technically alive but you are spiritually dead. Deprived of the refreshing waters of truth, life withers away when you stop growing.

A person who knows what they are doesn't necessarily want to know what will happen, because knowing itself is Being, the greatest joy, and what happens is determined by a vast conspiracy of factors over which individuals have minimal control. Everyone wants to live one more day. Don't conclude that you will die because of the second-hand information that bodies die. You need to wait to see if you disappear when your body falls. You were present before it appeared and you watch it leave you. You were never born. The Seer does not form conclusions. Seers are wonderstruck by the endless permutation and combinations of names and forms that present themselves within the scope of their panoramic awareness, and never conclude that they are real.

A journey without a goal, life is a timeless vacation through a partless land. Desiring the future and regretting the past, you are attempting to inject time into eternity. It never sticks. People who say they have arrived at truth have not arrived because they came to the conclusion that they have arrived. Conclusions don't apply, because you are immeasurable. You can't be packed into thought. Be sensible; keep learning until the day you seemingly die. Noticing, learning, investigating and appreciating are living states of mind which do not accumulate. Knowledge accumulates, cluttering and clouding the mind, the Self's window on the world. Yes, you may see but you see through a glass darkly.

Although *Sat Darshanam* was revealed by Ramana seventy years ago, and the *Kena Upanishad* was revealed seven thousand years ago by an unknown seer, the self-evident truth that both reveal is timeless.

Seeing is knowing that there is no connection between things, because there are no boundaries between things. Twelve hundred years ago, Gaudapada Maharshi humorously said that Vedanta is the *yoga* of no-contact, knowing full well that the word *yoga* means contact. You can't get in touch with your Self, because you are your Self. The truth is very simple, like space. To understand space, you don't need an advanced degree in physics. Simple observation will teach you everything you need to know.

It pervades everything. It is within and beyond all objects, very near and very far, like existence itself. Turn your attention toward it and see it shining in your Heart. Stare at objects and you will never apprehend it. It moves one step away when you take one step toward it.

When are you not experiencing yourself? It is your Self that seemingly wakes, dreams and sleeps, three states that include every possible experience. Never not present, it is your *svabhava*, your presence. You can't see it with your eyes, but you can feel it with your heart.

Seeing is not a thing, an idea or a process that you can initiate or imitate; it is the living presence of Being. It is knowing, which is not a thing or an action. You can say it is pure knowledge because without Awareness you don't know anything. You can only claim it as yourself. When are you not aware? The *Bhagavad Gita* says, "The one who sees, sees." Seeing is your nature, non-different from Being. Insentient objects like the body, emotions and thoughts come and go in your self-shining presence or they would not be known. You are never not present. Birth and death are beliefs that disappear when you see.

When your body first appears, you have no idea what it is. You are incorrectly informed by your caregivers that you are it, but it can't be you, because you see it. It dwells in you as you seemingly dwell in it. With it and without it you are you. When sleep removes waking, you aren't removed. You are present without a body. If you weren't, you wouldn't exist when waking removes sleep.

Commit to seeing and understand this timeless mystery that is not a mystery. Worship your feet as symbols of the knowing that stands under us. Transfer your identity to That. Say "I am" and fall silent. These words give birth to everything that is.

Accumulation

Life is seeing, Being, knowing. It does not accumulate. Thoughts and emotions accumulate. Collect them and go blind. But you need to know the difference between you and what you want before the teaching can work its magic. You can't remember What you are, because the one that remembers and forgets isn't you. You are present as you remember and forget. When you know this much, you have stepped on the path of learning. Words accumulate but learning is a state of mind that frees you from the tyranny of words. Words appear in the mirror of Vedanta, reveal your shining face, unlearn themselves and disappear.

Very often people separate because loving words are missing. Words are love, but love is not words. It is the non-dual bliss of Existence churning in the Heart no matter what the head is thinking. Feel it when the mind is uncluttered.

Loving, seeing, feeling, studying, surrendering to what appears and disappears, is the path.

Memories accumulate. An open mind is a bliss-filled mind; it needs no memories. Don't stuff the suitcase of your mind with happy thoughts as you travel to *nirvana*. When you accidently put your finger in a flame, you don't say "I know my finger is on fire." There is nothing to know. Just remove it because you have learned something.

Awareness as knowledge is not a thought. It is a telescope that brings what is hidden into focus, a living laser that concentrates the rays of the mind into the far corners of one's Being, exposing and destroying the ignorance lurking there.

You go to the dentist because your tooth aches, not because you think it aches. You pray because you have spotted a problem, and prayer removes it. It is something you have learned. You can call it knowledge, but thinking of it that way is dangerous. Your mind should be like a computer, always ignorant yet solving problems without the thought "I am solving problems." Learn how to see.

You are in a hurry to get to a city hundreds of miles away. At first you feel that you are moving quickly though the countryside, but after a while it feels as if you are sitting still and the road is passing under you. Miles become minutes and minutes become miles. Keep your mind on the goal, but know that when you think you are going somewhere you are going nowhere.

Duality: the Subject-Object Split

And why didn't you know that you weren't going anywhere when you began? Had you known, you would have taken your own sweet time, lingered at the rest stop, napped and explored a small village off the freeway. When you separate yourself from something, you are not looking at What Is. Separating yourself from your goal is called duality, an unnatural split bred of ignorance. To discover freedom and non-dual love, remove the subject-object split. But how?

Devotion

Devote yourself to Vedanta. It will teach you to see. Devotion is not a thought. It is a dynamic state of mind borrowed from Being that is always available, thanks to free will. Train your mind to hear the teachings as they are. Training is not a thought. It is a precious discipline. Don't allow your mind to interpret according to experiences real and imagined that you believe are knowledge. Allowing is not a thought. It is the spirit of renunciation. Empower your mind to say yes to what you don't wish to understand. Speaking truth is not a thought, it is living learning.

Thoughts are only powerful when you believe what you think. Belief is a conspiracy with ignorance. Ignorance is not a thought, it is not looking at What Is. Looking, inquiring, is not a thought. It is the nature of a curious mind. Curiosity is not a thought; it is your saving grace.

Vedanta sets your life rightside up, because not seeing has turned it upside down. You are not going here and there to collect souvenirs. Nothing can be added to you. How can you lose when nothing belongs to you in the first place? You arrive and leave in your birthday suit.

Listen like a child. And when you think about what you have heard like an adult, you learn. Because it is true to its object, Self-knowledge can never be dismissed so you can terminate your relationship with it. That I am is the truth. That I am full is a fact. That I see is the truth. Facts cannot be changed. They have no alternatives.

Isn't devoting myself to Vedanta just another goal? Am I not just prolonging the subject-object split? Yes, you are, but whereas the subject-object split is as good as non-existent, it is the grist for the mill of inquiry for the one who knows he doesn't know. Seeking is a deep crevice, a dark ravine. You cannot just jump out of it at will. You can, however, climb out happily, step by step, thought by thought. Climbing itself, which is not a thought, is the point. Climb and watch the ever-present, ever-realized goal that is not a goal emerge slowly from mists of misconception. Let us patiently expose your incestuous conspiracy with ignorance. We will teach you how to see, because you actually do see. Teaching is the shining light of truth.

I live in Spain and often go to Germany, where the walls of buildings serve as canvases for artists who paint scenes in the *trompe l'oeil* style, an artistic technique that tricks the eye into seeing something that isn't actually there. If the subject-object split is so deep that it feels natural, you may believe that the tradition – the teacher and the scripture – will eat your *karma*, stop your mind and make you know the truth, you are waiting before a wall with a painted door that will never open. It will not open, because you have unknowingly put yourself firmly on duality's subject side and the truth on the object side. The subject-object split exists or we wouldn't be talking about it, but it is as good as non-existent when the teaching subtly transfers the means of seeing to you. You are not a thing to be known.

You are so well known that nobody bothers to tell you that you exist and that you are conscious. But if you are lost deep in the Grand Canyon of ignorance, you need someone else to reveal your limitlessness, the uncaused happiness of Being, which is the nature of Existence. The plethora of non-dual books and videos cluttering the media today seductively and convincingly tout the special benefits of knowing who you are. Maybe you have been hypnotized by the insidious self-diminishing voice of ignorance and need to believe this message, but belief is cheap and easy. Children believe, first in Santa and the Tooth Fairy and later in absurd fantasies dressed up as facts, but if you're special, then everyone is special because there is only one of us.

Let go of your beliefs, and non-dual vision will spontaneously arise like a tender shoot from the inviting confines of the dark warm earth. Cultivate it assiduously with the living waters of this great teaching, the living word of God, or it will surely die.

A hundred years ago a *swami* invented "New Vedanta." In the middle of the last century another *swami* touted "Modern Vedanta," and toward the end Neo-Non-Duality and Evolutionary Spirituality, two additional chronocentric fantasies, sprouted. The world cannot be different, because it is not real. And if it was real, it couldn't be changed either. It is a value-neutral unchanging material principle, a thought. No paltry human movement, no messianic vision will transform it into utopia to forestall an inquiry into one's own fragmented inner world. I will not become a happier person because the world is a better place. I needed to feel unhappy because it seems so evil.

The teaching transcends labels; it is not traditional. It is timeless. You need it, because you are not ancient or modern. Like it, you too transcend time. Be very careful. Look and see if the certainty of your knowledge isn't just another belief born of a sense of entitled intellectual laziness gifted by an affluent society. Nowadays everyone craves the expedient, an easy path to instant enlightenment. If you hear that the Self-realized person kicks back and enjoys without doing, you may prematurely claim something that only comes from diligent hard work. If so, you have been infected by another duality, the doer-enjoyer split.

You need to give Being a chance to be, seeing the opportunity to see. You are working from womb to tomb whether you know it or not. Activity is the signature of the living energy of Being. You do what you do for one reason only: you want to enjoy yourself. Not knowing that you are the joy, you want to enjoy.

See the irony. Action is inescapably factual, not conceptual. Forget your fantasies. See what is required and participate.

See the Is-ness, Not the Thought-ness

Problems are never about people, places, activities, situations and things; they are always about our mental/emotional selves, our likes and dislikes. If joy was in objects, the same object would give joy to everyone.

Comparison is the thief of joy. The world can never compare to the ideal world of our imagination. Every transactional experience comes up short. The mind is binary, locked in duality, dwelling on qualities and categories, setting up one thing against another, juxtaposing this and that. Look at life through the mind if you want to go blind. Think a thought and think a thought about the thought if you want to suffer. You will suffer unless you scrutinize your thoughts and feelings in light of What you are, Existence shining as Awareness.

Your experiences are just you, ever-present ordinary Awareness and the thought playing in your mind at the moment. Subtract the thought, and you are Awareness. And because you like certain experiences and dislike others, each thought is accompanied by an emotion, and these emotions cause your body to motor toward or run from this or that situation in the "real" world, not knowing that you are only chasing another acceptable thought or trying to avoid an unpleasant idea.

This whole process makes you experience-rich and you may imagine that you are really living because you are so busy and have accumulated so much experience. But complicated, abstracted conceptual richness is not life, because you are living a second away from What Is, a painful millimeter apart from your Self. This worldly state of mind is not real, no matter how much you mouth the words. You are the non-attached Seer, and the world is only the play of your imagination.

The Apparent Reality

This fact has been known for a long time. The likelihood of meaningfully enjoying the world is more or less the equivalent of a camel, which is a big animal with a big belly, trying to successfully wiggle through the eye of a needle. However, the What Is that is you is joyful richness itself. The paltry reflected pleasures that momentarily blink on and off like faraway stars with every passing experience shine after you. Unborn, you shine first and you shine alone.

Shankara's great statement that Awareness is real and the world is apparently real is not a statement to be memorized and repeated like a *mantra*. You are not seeing reality when you are looking at the world through its image in your mind, because you are separating it from yourself. You are not seeing objectively through the lens of your eyes, like a camera. When you look at the past, you don't see the present. Looking at the future, you destroy the present. The whole mental process is only seemingly real, like a movie, a dream.

What you see is apparently real, *mithya*. The eyesight that reveals the flower is *mithya*; the mind which categorizes the rose as a flower is *mithya*; the combination of the knower and the known is *mithya*; the sun, moon, stars and the whole cosmos is *mithya*, all very near but very far from the truth. Don't imagine that *mithya* is some exotic thing that is only understood by ancient cave-dwelling sages. Everybody experiences it every minute of every day. It is just normal life. Discrimination, which handles *mithya*, is the fact that the objective world is not real, and the fishy conceptual person swimming in it is only a dream person.

How to "See" What Is When What Is Sees?

Getting back to What Is is difficult, because What Is can't be objectified. Furthermore, standing up to the habit of engaging in What Isn't requires considerable alertness, not to mention that it's challenging and sometimes deadly boring. When you first hear the teaching, it is difficult to easily accept the simple truthful counter-intuitive statement that your body and mind aren't you, much less later when you told that it is you – but you aren't it! You may think the teaching, which keeps jumping back and forth from one perspective to another, is absurd. Perhaps you just want something simple, something to do, a practical formula you can remember and repeat when you're not happy. Your mind is probably worn out from years of emotion and wants to rest. But you may have to unravel lifetimes of unthinking before you really wake up.

When you first became aware of words, even before you knew what they meant, your mother said, "That is a dog, a cat, a tree, a house." You didn't know you were your body; it was just another strange object among many, but when she used the word "that" and pointed to the dog, the idea of space, distance, only worked if you were the body. You didn't infer, but inference inferred it for you. It had a certain logic and your unconscious mind bought into it. Or when she caught you fiddling with your privy parts years later, she said, "Don't touch yourself," even though in this case the connection between yourself and your manhood is pretty sketchy. Over and over, day in and day out, the world supplied a "this" for every "that" and the small crack in your mind became a deep ravine. What is more obvious than the fact that what you see can't be you? Yet, when someone touches your body inappropriately, you say, "Don't touch me." It becomes an orientation, completely unconscious.

The Discipline

You've had your insights and epiphanies large and small, but resting as – not in – Being is not a one-off. You need to fight a very clever hidden adversary that pits you against yourself, which usually takes years of practice. It is not easy to stand up to the mind, speak truth to its insidious power and not allow it to relentlessly push its agenda. At first it will sullenly, sometimes violently, resist but it will eventually come around if you take the long-term view and patiently bring it to heel. Such is its nature that it is never sure if it should be a friend or an enemy, so you need to counsel it and be prepared for ups and downs.

Let your physical eyes become a conduit for the inner light, because the eyes themselves are not troubled by the knower-known division. Subtract the non-essential – body, mind, senses and the world – and appreciate your Is-ness. Not to worry, you can't subtract you. Being is Seeing because Existence and Awareness are non-different. They are What Is. There is only Seeing-Being.

The knower and the known are made of the same substance, like the ocean and its waves. They are never not present. Keep the mind out of it, but don't suppress it. Let it jabber and blabber like a schoolchild. It can't help it. If it could be different, it would. Pity it, comfort it, be amused and entertained. Abide, without abiding, as the Seer. And, insofar as you tire of its meaningless chatter, give it a good whack now and then.

II

Invocation

What is the Existence Principle that pervades all objects, all names and forms and the experiencing subject? Without it no experiences are possible. It is the witnessing Awareness Principle shining as the essence of the Mind, and is called the Heart. It is the only limitless, divisionless, non-dual Principle. Because it is not an object of thought, it cannot be known by the experiencing subject. To know It is to abide in It without objectifying It. [1]

EVERY DAY I wake up and look out the window at a spectacular landscape from the top of a mountain in the Axarquia Mountains in southern Spain. I draw the curtains and pinch myself to make sure I'm awake because I feel a great sense of dreamlike wonder and gratitude that whatever moves us here and there through life daily sees fit to pleasure the eyes of an old man in his sunset years with unspeakable beauty and his ears with the equally unspeakable silence of eternity.

On the edge of a nearby ridge sits a big boxy house with perhaps a slightly more commanding view. My mind hates that house with a passion but not for long, however, because the next thought invokes a feeling of wonder akin to the sensation inspired by the panorama of granite peaks and undulating hills that accommodate a vast patchwork of almond and olive farms stretching south for thirty miles that end at the bottom of a huge mountain obscuring the view of the Mediterranean on the other side.

For reasons known only to the prime mover, my mind has been blessed (perhaps cursed is a better word) with a refined sense of aesthetics. To call the house boxy isn't quite right, because "boxy" implies that it may contain other more interesting features. To my sensibilities, it doesn't. It's a big box. I suppose when you get right down to it a box is a box is a box, so you can't say one is more or less beautiful than another, unless you are uplifted by an ornate gift box from a high-end retailer of chocolates, perfumes or bespoke footwear. The mind, performing its predictable function, craves to criticize the big boxy house with yet another negative thought, but I know better and move to silence.

I choose to no longer allow the mind to dwell on its biases. Yet a different type of wonder returns, invoked by the thought that this box sports three postage-stamp-sized windows depriving the occupants – whom never seem to visit – of a most spectacular view. This box fills me with wonder because I can't fathom how anyone with eyes could fail to install a generous bank of windows which the view truly demands. God's glory begs to be seen. Do I dwell on the absentee owners or an untalented and perhaps harried contractor? You might say my query is vanity, but God wants to be seen.

And yet – only the one who sees sees what is hidden in plain sight. The Existence principle that shines as Awareness is like space insofar as it pervades every one of our experiences, the variegated and limitless sentient and insentient world of names and forms that make up the world and the apparent person we have been told we are. Its nature is limitless bliss, and yet who sees it? Like gravity it is as old as the hills, present everywhere and hidden in plain sight but how many gravity-thoughts does one have during one's lifespan? The one non-binary thing that will make us infinitely richer than Jeff Bezos provides more intense pleasure than football and puts a spring in our step is unknown – for want of another kind of "eye."

The mind is an "eye" that opens up the world of names and forms to the secret Existence principle sitting silently behind it. But this "eye" can't keep its "mouth" shut. From womb to tomb it yammers and stammers, jabbers and blabbers, natters and chatters, rants and raves. Not only will it not sit still, it is cursed with greed. It wants more, more, more, better, better, better and different, different, different. It wants quantity, quality, variety and novelty – and it wants it NOW! It is driven by an insatiable hunger for experiences that are meant to make it feel secure, satisfied, powerful, famous, virtuous and respectable. And yet we love the mind, at least as much as we do our spouses and our darling bundles of juvenile joy, and probably more.

But as Ganapathi Muni, the wise Tamil poet who rendered Ramana's text in Sanskrit, says, "Because the witnessing Consciousness principle is not an object of thought, It cannot be known by the experiencing subject. To know It is to abide in It without objectifying It." "Because It is not an object of thought" means that experience is nothing but our yammers and stammers rising and falling in the light of Existence appearing as our ordinary Awareness. And therein lies the rub. We stare at the world like hypnotized zombies expecting it to deliver lasting bliss, and all it can come up with is a few paltry moments of zero-sum pleasure interspersed with sometimes tediously expanded periods of suffering.

> Can there be the feeling of "I" without that which exists always
> free from thoughts, it exists, this inner being, the Heart?
> How then to know that which is beyond the mind?
> To know it is to abide firmly in the Heart. [2]

We're missing the mark, because we're focused on the "I-sense," popularly known as the ego. It is the part of you that identifies with thoughts, emotions and activities. It is a subtle, seemingly conscious, reflective abstraction that superficially resembles the Existence principle, but is dependent on it. Just as physical, psychological and moral principles structure our daily lives, the Existence principle structures all the seen and unseen names and forms that comprise the experience of everything and everyone.

Each and every experience presupposes a prior universal Consciousness/ Awareness that is so very present and intimately available that it is never included in our day-to-day consideration of the world and of ourselves. It is not considered and included, because it is mislabeled as a virtual Facebook-style entity, an "avatar" of sorts, with a fictitious birthday and cooked-up name. Furthermore, it is burdened with memory, a future, a raft of instruments of knowledge and experience and loaded with *karma* to keep it distracted from what it really is, the Existence principle, the "Heart." Ramana calls this impos-ter the "I-sense."

If the Existence principle is not a discrete experience beyond experience and knowledge, do I need to go to another world to experience it? Vedanta and Ramana emphatically say no. Every time you say or think the word "I" you unwittingly refer to it. We are never not experiencing the Existence principle, which Ramana metaphorically calls "abiding in the Heart." "To know It is to abide in It without objectifying It" means that it is not an object but the very essence of the mislabeled experiencer.

> The "I" thought is the first to die for those who have taken refuge,
> out of fear of death, at the feet of Shiva, the conqueror of death!
> Thereafter, they are naturally immortal.
> Can they ever again be assailed by the fear of death?
> Therefore, worship Shiva. [3]

If you want to stop worrying about change, which is symbolized by the word "death," the "I-sense" or "I-thought" has to die. In other words, it requires the death of the ego. Fortunately, that death has nothing to do with you, because the I, non-binary Existence shining as Consciousness, is immortal. The forty verses that follow unfold the science of Existence shining as Consciousness, or Awareness, if you prefer.

Before we delve into the text, we need to clarify what does not apply in this context, namely a definition of ego that refers to the pride and willful ignorance that claims ownership of things that belong to God. Next, we need to dismiss the clumsy, ill-conceived popular notion of ego death, which is based on the notion that the "I-sense" prevents us from experiencing bliss of the I, which is not true. Asking an embodied being to kill itself is absurd because it would only do so if it thought that it would be present to enjoy the results of its actions, which it won't if it's dead. Furthermore, the "I-thought" is not actually conscious insofar as it is a notion, and notions are inert, which makes them incapable of action. So on both counts the idea comes up short. The death Ramana speaks of is the death of an idea, which is accomplished by abiding in the Heart, which will be explained as we proceed.

Existence Shining As Awareness

Because we see the variegated world, a single source
with unlimited powers must be accepted.
The seer, the seen and the substrate
on which it is projected – the Light –
are all only He, the One. [1]

All religions are based on the existence
of the individual, the world and God.
So long as individuality lasts,
these three remain separate.
To abide, egoless, in the Self, is the best. [2]

In keeping with the *Upanishads*, the source texts, all Vedic sages say the world's myriad forms must have a single source. The world is a consciously designed matrix, which is seemingly different but not actually different from the intelligence that generates it. If there were more than one source, there would be more than one organizing principle, the world would be a chaos and we would not get out of bed in the morning, because purposeful work would be impossible. Only Existence shining as Awareness has the power to create the world. One undivided painted canvas appears as the many objects portrayed on it. The Creation is comprised of three factors: a conscious subject; a material medium which generates subtle inner experiences and gross material objects with which the conscious subject interacts; and a substratum, non-dual Existence, on which "variegated names and forms" are projected.

19

There is a seeming difference, not an actual difference, between the projected forms and the substrate, just as there is no difference between the words appearing on a monitor and the pixels that generate them. The words "at the feet of Shiva" in verse three implies a difference between the worshiper and God, insofar as God doesn't have feet. The word "feet" is a metaphorical reference to Existence because Existence "stands under" all sentient and insentient objects, just as the feet uphold the body, which is to say it supports the world and everything in it. In this case the word "Shiva" means "that which is good anytime in all circumstances," not the blue-necked Hindu god Shiva. What could that be but Existence itself insofar as the person you think you are doesn't exist without it? The capitalized pronoun "He" is also metaphorical, insofar as God is an impersonal principle, not a big person or an energetic force situated elsewhere.

Dualistic religions assume two eternal principles: an eternal soul encapsulated in a material body and an eternal external God, for which there is no evidence apart from a belief, which is only evidence of itself. An internal soul implies a second thing, as does an external God. If one thing depends on another, it is seemingly real at best, which implies that it is not real at all. And insofar as this apparent living entity lives on borrowed existence, it will have to relinquish its life one fine day. Furthermore, if two or more eternal principles exist, which one is real?

Being sentient, the "I-sense" is capable of feeling that it is divided and it is equally capable of believing that it was created previously by someone or something, but belief is, well, not fact. The feeling of duality contradicts experience because only one Self experiences the feeling of being two or more selves. If there were two or more of us, we would have two or more identity cards. We imagine that there are others because we associate Being with a specific material sheath, which is actually only a single material medium appearing as many. If you associate Being with matter, you will naturally think that you decay and die, because that's what matter does.

Ramana says that if you want to remove conflict and the worry of non-existence, negate your ego (*ahamkara*), the dualistic experiencing entity, and establish your identity as Existence shining as Awareness, the non-dual principle. You are a What, not a who.

> What use are disputes such as "The world is real,"
> "No, it is a mirage," "It is conscious energy,"
> "No, it is matter," "Life is joy," "No, it is sorrow,"

20

"There is no self," "There is a self"?
Abidance in the exalted state
where neither the ego nor the world exists
is acceptable to all. [3]

An inquiry into whether the world is real or not is pointless, because the world only exists for you when you are thinking the world-thought. Where is it when you are thinking some other thought? You never saw a world apart from the thought of it. And even if you could objectively know the world at one moment, the knowledge would be useless the next, because the world is never the same from one nanosecond to the other. Loved ones love you when they think they love you and don't love you when they think they don't. Furthermore, because the idea of a world holds out the carrot of happiness, the ego, which also only exists when you are conscious of it, has a vested interest in non-inquiry into the world. When it feels incomplete, it erroneously believes that the world provides experiences that can fulfill it. And when it is satisfied, it does not need the blandishments of the world at all. The ego, an imposter if ever there was one, is a flimsy identity hastily concocted out of a biased interpretation of actual and imaginary past happenings that bolster its concept of itself.

If the world is not a fit subject of inquiry, then inquiry into God is equally useless for the same reasons. What is your God apart from your thought of God? Where is it when you are thinking of your wife and kids? Neither the world nor God supply answers, because they are remote impersonal principles that our limited minds are incapable of understanding unless they are reduced to simple concepts. That some individuals are satisfied and others aren't is due to the results of their actions, not divine will or luck. Inquiry into one's sense of individuality from the non-dual platform is the best way to remove duality. Ramana asks us to inquire into the ego because it is nearest and dearest to us. Proper inquiry negates the "I-sense" and results in the non-dual "state" (*nistha*) of steady wisdom in which there are no divisions and no localized "I-sense."

As the mind, so the world.

So long as one thinks one has a form,
the world and God have form.
When one is the formless Self, who is there to see?
He or she is the Seer, complete and limitless. [4]

21

The way you look at God is the way you look at yourself. So leave God out of it and seek to know your non-eternal self. Knowing it is removing it because it is as good as non-existent in the first place. Once it is removed, "the Seer shines in all its glory," which doesn't mean that it wasn't shining before, only that is has been uncovered. Inquiry just removes the idea that the "I-sense" is your identity, which obscures the view, which is not a view, of you. Vedanta is not self-improvement. How can you change something that isn't real?

There is only ever one unchanging Seer seeing itself, and it is you, even when you are ignorant of it.

The light sees the darkness, but the darkness sees not the light.

> The body is made up of five sheaths.
> It and the world coexist.
> Can anyone see the world
> unless he has a body? [5]

Without the belief "I am the fivefold body," how can the world appear? Even if it does appear it is unreal, because it depends on the existence of the body. The body is equally unreal and therefore unreliable as a means of happiness, because it depends on the world for its existence.

If you know the teachings of Vedanta, you may think you are superior to worldly people or take pride in your growth, which is arrogance. If you know the glory of *Isvara*, you may play the humble devotee, which is reverse arrogance, which perhaps makes you look good in your own eyes and the eyes of others. But feeling good is not the point, since you are goodness itself prior to all your feelings. Seeing What you are entitles you to legitimately worship your Self; you are the goodness that makes goodness good. When you know you are What Is, you can only say "I am Existence shining as Awareness" because What you are cannot be evaluated. You are the value of everything that the "I-sense" values.

The Living Processes of Being

The blade of truth is seemingly hidden in the scabbard of the human personality, which has several layers. The layers are the living processes of Being. Traditionally they are presented as three "bodies": the gross body; the subtle body; and the causal body. Ramana lists five "sheaths," another traditional categorization. They are: (1) the "food sheath," or the physical body; (2) the vital air sheath, or the physiological systems; (3) the mind, or emotional sheath; (4) the intellect, or thought sheath; and (5) the bliss sheath, or the happiness sheath.

No one you meet knows that they are non-different from unborn non-dual Existence shining as Awareness, because their attention, which is reflected awareness, is fixated on one of these layers of experience all the time. Although it does, the scabbard doesn't actually hide the blade of truth; you don't see the blade, but you know it is in the scabbard because a handle implies a blade. Vedanta presents the sum total of our experiences in this structured conceptual way to impress your mind as to their importance for the process of discrimination, which is good insofar as you need to understand the tools you have at your disposal as you try to steer your little ship safely across the seemingly changing ocean of Existence.

When you think of a tool, however, you usually think of a static material object like a hammer, a screwdriver or a saw. My teacher referred to them as "equipment," an effective metaphor that conveys the idea that knowledge of them is useful for a freedom-seeker. Even though this is true, it tends to make an inquirer think they are inert intellectual categories, which is also true. However, metaphors don't tell the whole story; they conceal certain facts as they reveal others. The static nature of the tool-sheath-equipment metaphors hides the fact that they are actually dynamic processes of Being, not just static, collectable, memorizable concepts.

So I have rejigged the categories and the language a little to make the point that you need to understand and relate to them practically, not just intellectually, on a moment-to-moment basis. Why? Because they are your life. You are not a category, a memory or a thought. Your life is not a category, a memory or a thought. Yes, Vedanta is as precise and rigorous as any material science and more rigorous than social, psychological and political sciences, but you are not here to study Vedanta. You are here to study your "I-sense" with Vedanta's help because it is not only the sole gateway to freedom and non-dual love, it is the biggest impediment to freedom and non-dual love. Because it is the nearest and dearest topic to all sentient beings, we should understand it in the best possible way.

If you say, "I thought you were going to teach us the Self," I'm sorry to disappoint you, but I can't teach you the Self, because the Self is not an object of knowledge. We don't give you knowledge, we take ignorance away. Well, that's not really true either. We give knowledge of what you aren't, which removes ignorance about it, and then we remove knowledge, leaving you as pure as the driven snow.

You can't know What you are like you know a tree or a bird. Knowledge doesn't move from the unknown to the known. It always starts with a known something and then moves on to discover an unknown something. Like material sciences, and in fact the human mind itself, Vedanta extrapolates. However, in its case you rediscover something you already knew but didn't know you knew.

You may believe you will "find yourself" though your experiences, but nothing hides us from ourselves like experiences. You only experience what you aren't. Out of Existence shining as Awareness – experience arises. Consequently you know what you are experiencing. You know just how depressed or elated you are. You know every single step on the path up the mountain of desire and every single step down its fear side. You keep a journal: "I did this. Then I did that." The real "I" is present, no doubt, but like a camera it never shows up in the photograph. Your life is lifeless unless the real you is included in the picture. Sadly, what's happening is the only topic of interest because it is never the same from one moment to the next and I NEED TO BE SECURE. ALWAYS!

The good old days when you could while away time in idle pursuits are dead and gone. We have things to do, places to go and people to meet. Every waking hour we are riveted to our spendy little info screens. Their annoying self-important beeps incessantly update us on topics too numerous to mention so we can get the edge on life before it gets the edge on us. What is happening, not What I am, is seemingly our only concern. If you google "What am I?" there is only one result, not two hundred fifty-three thousand; you are a consumer of experience. If you don't appreciate that you are the "happening" needed for happenings to happen, you can easily waste your whole life pursuing experiences that are dead before they die.

Living Processes

You probably never thought about it much, but everything every conscious being has learned since the first sense organ stuck its eyeball out of the gaseous Precambrian swamp billions of years ago to see what was happening is in you now. Zillions of entities tirelessly confronted life and developed the autonomic processes that work ceaselessly behind the scenes to keep the body functioning. Evolution is your friend. Appreciate its legacy.

It also evolved our emotional self, establishing the binary template of emotions that pull you toward appealing situations and cause you to run from danger – your fears and desires. Once the basic internal set-up was in place, it refined the fears and desires into a great variety of gross and subtle likes and dislikes. What were once luxuries less than a century ago are now considered necessities by a large percentage of humans. We have become a world of princesses who can't get a good night's sleep, because their mobile device is out of energy and the electricity grid is down due to an unexpected storm.

We like pets and babies because they are powered exclusively by built-in processes that keep them from self-conscious thinking and allow Existence shining as Awareness to bring joy to our lives and remind us of what we once were. Simple and straightforward, they aren't cluttered, complicated and constipated with concepts. What you see is what you get because they trust that everything is exactly as it should be and are joyous in it. They are authentic and non-dual. For a short while they are unburdened by ego, but soon enough they pick up our worries and become just like us, fraught with the problems of children. If you think about it a little, there is no particular reason why you can't remember this simple way of Being and learn to trust yourself.

Thirdly, evolution gifted us with intellect reflected in the size and complexity of the human brain, a blob of fat between the ears. The ancient taxonomists settled on the word *manusha* for humans, a Sanskrit term meaning variously "the ones that think; mind; and man." Every sentient entity is blessed or cursed with fear and desire. Mindless cockroaches scatter when you turn on the kitchen light, and even plants lean toward the sun. But the plant and animal kingdom is worry-free; human beings, not so much.

Again, we are blessed with perception, cognition, self-reflection, inference and discrimination. Of course we aren't our bodies and minds, but we need to see them for what they are before we see ourselves as we really are. So the intellect is a wonderful tool indeed; with the help of a scientific impersonal investigative means it can pick the lock of our mental prison and open our minds to the limitless freedom of existence if it has the code. But unless we study the user manual and employ it properly, it can incarcerate us in a hellish prison of raging emotions.

To show how disconnected from the processes that support us, we say "I know the tree" instead of "I'm cognizing the tree," which means that the life in me and the life in the tree are connected. I have a living relationship with trees because we are both alive. If I am connected to dead concepts, I'm as good as dead myself.

The world appears when you wake up.

Even though the mind and the world
rise and set together, the mind illumines the world.
The light from which they arise and into which they set
is the Reality, which does not arise and subside. (7)

Is the world there because I see it or do I see it because it is there? The world and the mind appear simultaneously, so there is no cause-and-effect relationship. However, because the mind illumines the world, it is said to be the cause of the world for the purposes of leading the inquirer back to the source.

You can count on knowledge.

Worshiping the Supreme in any name or form
is an aid for the vision of It.
True vision, however, is merging
and abiding in the Reality. (8)

Karma yoga is an indirect means, and firm knowledge is the direct means, of liberation. Abiding in reality is claiming the living non-dual vision awakened by the teaching. "Merging," "abiding" and "state" are dualistic words implying action, which do not address ignorance, the actual problem. So we have to assume that he is using them figuratively to convey knowledge, the non-separation of the seeker and the sought. Although he was a non-dual wise person, he practiced dualistic devotion of Shiva in the form of a holy mountain, which only goes to show that non-dual wisdom and dualistic love are not in conflict. Love is love.

From the individual's perspective, a state of knowledge is always available and reliable, whereas a state of experience is unreliable and intermittently available. As Shankara says in *Atma Bodha*, "Experience prepares the food. Knowledge cooks it."

When the individual, for whom the subject and
its objects exist and the means of knowledge exist,
is investigated, both prove to be seemingly real.
Then all mental movement ceases forever. (9)

26

The investigation Ramana speaks of is the signature practice of Vedanta, *atma-anatma viveka*, sorting the unchanging awareness portion of the "I-sense" from the apparently real reflecting medium, the material portion. For want of discrimination, an individual is uncertain whether it's a spiritual entity with a material portion or a material entity with occasional spiritual impulses. When you look into your relationship with objects, you're unable to discern if you, the conscious subject, depend on the inert objects you experience or the inert objects that you experience – thoughts and feelings, for instance – depend on you. When you get it right, "all mental movement" with regard to this fundamental confusion "ceases forever."

The ever-free conscious subject employs three means of knowledge: a knowing intellect; a feeling heart; and sense organs. All three are material instruments, which only exist if they are known to exist. There are no objects of knowledge if the conscious subject is not present, so what you know and experience depends on you, not the other way around. What a relief!

"Mental movement" means worry, not a blank mind. If all mental movement stopped forever, then how did Ramana write this *Upanishad*, not to mention live a normal life? It means the Self is thought-free. Thoughts continue by the grace, some say will, of *Isvara/Maya*, the creative factor that generates the seemingly real world. To say thoughts stop means thought is *mithya*, apparently real, not actually real. They are not real for a wise person. For a person who doesn't know what he or she is, they are real.

The world of our experience is always a mixture, like a rope that appears as a snake, or a mirage in the desert. The snake's existence is sustained by ignorance of the rope.

The jury is not out on who we are. In fact "Who am I?" is not the right question. "What am I?" is correct insofar as thinking of one's Self as a unique individual subject to *karma* causes suffering. Inquiry is a living vision brought about by an unbiased hearing of the teaching.

The scripture, which is the words of the "Supreme," says, "You are unborn limitless non-dual Existence shining as Awareness, not this limited body-mind assemblage." Inquiry is exposing the mind to this teaching and evaluating the ego/mind's beliefs and opinions with reference to it, bolstered by scripture-inspired confidence and common-sense observation that the individual and its accumulated experience-based knowledge are not real. Our beliefs and opinions cause conflict with What Is and need to be removed.

Can knowledge exist without ignorance?
Can ignorance exist without knowledge?

27

Investigating the source of the individual to whom
they pertain and abiding there is true knowledge. [10]

An untaught individual doesn't chose between knowledge and ignorance until he or she knows what constitutes both, because *jivas* always think that what they believe to be true is true, whether it is or not. Therefore an individual's "knowledge" is always suspect, until it has heard the teachings. Once it gains access to the Self's point of view, it can objectively evaluate its beliefs and opinions, with the intention of discarding those that are not actually knowledge.

Knowledge and ignorance are mutually exclusive dualities. If you were living on the sun, you wouldn't know what darkness is, so you would have no word for light. If there were only women on the earth, there would be no word for men. You can't blame yourself for what you don't know, but once you hear that you are non-separate from the fullness of Existence, and by extension non-different from everything that seems to be different, you are willfully ignorant if you don't discard the vision of duality.

Knowledge is true to the object of knowledge.

Can knowledge of any object,
without Self-knowledge, be true knowledge?
Knowledge of the Self, which is the support of knower and known,
destroys knowledge and ignorance. [11]

If you are knowledge-oriented but don't know what you are, you have no choice but to seek knowledge of what you aren't. Knowledge of objects will not solve the "What am I?" issue. So remove ignorance with knowledge and remove knowledge by dropping into the Heart, meaning accepting your identity as Existence/Awareness, which is beyond knowledge. Self-knowledge is the Self's only access to itself because knowledge is true to its object. Knowledge of inert objects directs one's living vision to dying things and consigns one's life, which is little better than death without Self-knowledge, to a decaying conceptual world.

Self-knowledge is "I am limitless, unborn, ever-present, whole and complete Existence/Awareness." It is knowing what it means to say "I am" in light of the ego's experience of objects. It is knowing that the true I is not the "I-sense."

Drop into the Heart and take a stand in What Is.

....

Neither sleep nor the cognition of objects is knowledge.

In the true state, which is different from both,

in Awareness there are no objects. It shines alone.

Hence it is not a void. [12]

Waking-state worldly knowledge is obtained through a process of learning that reveals something that was previously unknown, but Self-knowledge does not reveal an unknown object. A thought is required for knowledge of objects, but the Self is not an object and the Self does not think, so Self-knowledge is Awareness because Awareness is the thought-free "object." To distinguish it from thought-knowledge, Ramana calls it the true state (*nishta*) because it is not subject to dismissal. There is no knowledge in deep sleep, only the immediate experience of limitlessness and bliss, because the intellect is dormant in sleep.

Because Awareness is not an object of knowledge, people assume that it is nothingness. Nothingness is non-existent, like the horns of rabbits. If there were an existent category called nothing, it could only be known if Awareness was present, which means that it doesn't exist, apart from the thought of non-existence, which means that it isn't real.

Self-knowledge is a loss of ignorance, not a gain of knowledge.

....

Self-knowledge is dropping the misconception about one's identity brought about by exposing the mind to the teaching. Exposing the mind is listening without the interference of conditioned biases. I "get" What I am when I understand that I can't "get" What I am, because I already am it. It is not something new. Self-knowledge is "I am free because I am Existence shining as Awareness. I was never bound." When you hear the truth, you are not amazed at it, you are amazed that you could have missed something so simple and obvious. That the Self is not known to be unknown is the problem, because we misidentify it as a conceptual self.

Existence is called knowledge when it is associated with a thought.

....

Awareness, the Self, is real.

Names and forms cannot exist apart from it.

Can seemingly different ornaments exist apart from gold? [13]

29

Existence alone appears in the form of different types of knowledge. Existence is called knowledge when it is associated with a thought. It is called experience when it is associated with a perception, a process. Processes are eternal living streams of thought activated by the power of Awareness.

Thought-knowledge is not real, and the knowledge "I am Awareness" is also not real, but it is enough to cancel the unreal "I-sense," assuming certain qualifications, to which Ramana alludes when he recommends worship of Shiva, which symbolizes various preparatory practices, *karma yoga*, for instance. *Karma yoga* is worship, offering one's actions to the world in a spirit of love, which reduces an individual's attachment to its "me-sense" and sets the stage for *jnana yoga*, the knowledge that destroys the idea that the "I-sense" is one's real identity.

"Real" means never-not-present non-dual existence. Knowledge and ignorance are mutually dependent concepts. When one is present, the other isn't.

> Without the "I" the second and third persons cannot exist.
>
> When the "I" subsides during enquiry into its source,
>
> the second and third persons disappear
>
> and our natural state shines forth. (14)

The "I-sense" is the root of all problems. It creates the transactional reality and consigns an individual to a life of continual struggle. A wise person has an ego, but it is known to be "not-Self," a seemingly real object. An ignorant person associates Awareness with the body. Thinking he depends on the body as he searches happiness, he irrationally pursues objects and comes to grief, whereas a wise person is self-controlled because he knows the body exists by his grace. He or she enjoys objects but withdraws the senses when danger approaches, like a turtle withdraws its limbs.

How can I have problems with you if there is no "me"? Stepping away from me means stepping into What Is because there is no other option. Non-duality means that I experience through all bodies and minds, just as one electricity powers myriad devices. I am not opposed to anything. I am like space. Fill me with myriad transforming objects and I remain unchanged.

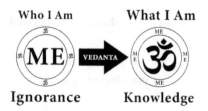

30

The first person is not the Me.

The first ten verses of the *Bhagavad Gita* begin with a description of the Me-self, which, like a silk worm, incarcerates itself in a binding cocoon of desires and fears that become a prison of delusion and despair. The Me-self is an object created by your memory identified with subjective events, material objects and external situations. Your actual Self, blissful Existence shining as Awareness, is limitless, but when you obsess on the Me-self, you discover that you are imprisoned by time and conclude that you will die one day, which definitely takes the edge off life. If you can dismantle this ersatz identity, you "become" immortal and your worries cease.

Accumulation

There was a holy man with only one pair of underwear, which he laundered regularly in the river. A friend observed this and convinced him to get a second pair because it was improper to appear naked in public. He complained that taking care of a second pair took time away from his meditation, so his friend suggested he get a wife, who could attend to his laundry, which he did. It soon became apparent, however, that he would have to feed his wife, which sent him begging for food for several hours a day, which further ate into his meditation time. So the friend suggested that he get a cow and a chicken for milk and eggs to feed her, which he did. But the wife was bored because he was always away collecting money and continually whining that he didn't have time for meditation, so she insisted on having two children to amuse her. There is not sufficient room in this document to chronicle the remainder of our hero's life, so I will cut to the chase. The moral is: when your Me-self is the center of your life, you think you need to control everything to get what you want, so you work like a demon and lose your peace of mind, but if you understand that *Isvara* is the controller, the center dissolves, the worry goes and you gain limitless bliss.

Karma Yoga and Jnana Yoga

When you pull a yo-yo toward you, the string wraps tightly around the center, but when you throw it away, the string unravels and the tension disappears. Anxiety disappears as *karma yoga* unravels and neutralizes the Me's likes and

31

dislikes. The more you accumulate subjectively and objectively the bigger the center grows and the more the periphery recedes until escape is impossible. As you drop accumulated thoughts, the center shrinks and eventually vanishes. If there is no center, there is no periphery. *Jnana yoga*, Self-inquiry, is dropping the erroneous notions and beliefs that wind us into constipated balls of frustration. Standing as the "I am" strips the thoughts of meaning and they fall helplessly away.

You can live without desires but you can't live without groceries. When the center vanishes, you are still the same person. The family, job, bank account and the house remain. Your duties continue. You go to work and pay the rent, but these things are enjoyable, because you are blessed with a tremendous enthusiasm when the center dissolves.

Hedged Love - Attachment

You love yourself when you sleep because there is no center. Where there is no center, there is only love, so you enjoy yourself absolutely. But when you wake up, your love is hedged. It goes to my children, my wife, my parents, my friends, my house, my garden, my job and my religion. When I am driving, I am driving *a* car, not *my* car. Which part of the car did I make? If you are the author of something, you can claim ownership, but if you think about it, the constituents of everything that you value – your "I-sense" and its powers of perception, cognition and action – belong to *Isvara*, not to mention everything else in the whole blessed universe. We are all second-hand people. Johnny-come-latelies, we show up when the party is over. God had all the fun.

But *karma yoga* and *jnana yoga* are means operated by the Me-self, which implies an end, which makes the Me-self a slave to time and space. Although I'm free, I wonder when I will be free. Truth, however, is timeless, so methods don't work. What to do? Seeing that you are already seeing dismantles the mind in one go, and you immediately begin to live large.

It is a laughing matter to debate about
the past and future, because they are only thoughts in the present.
Can you count to two without the number one? [15]

There is no past apart from the concept of the past. If the past was actual, you could experience it. It completely depends on the present. When yesterday existed, it was called the present, which is pure imagination. When the future happens, it will be called the present. Even the present doesn't exist, because it depends on the presence of two equally non-existent factors, the past and the future. If something depends on a non-existent something, does it exist?

However, the "present" is a useful word because of its association with the word "presence," which refers to an actual something: you, Existence. A deaf and blind person experiences the presence of another deaf and blind person in the room. Presence knows presence. Consequently it is said that only a wise person knows a wise person.

If time and space depend on me and I don't depend on anything, then I am free of time and space. That I think I am time-and-space-bound is due to the misconception that I am the body-mind-sense complex. Yesterday is a name for memory. Tomorrow is a name for the fiction that life "continues." Life doesn't continue, because it never started. It is eternal. It is just another name for Existence. When you say you are alive, you actually mean that you are ever-free Awareness. You live without breathing. Life and death, like the past, future and present, are only concepts. Because they exist, you can take them as Awareness and stop pretending that you were born and that you will die.

> Can there be space or time apart from me?
> Space and time bind me only if I am the body.
> I am nowhere, I am timeless,
> I exist everywhere and always. (16)

When there is an "I-sense" there are problems. Why meditate on it? When there is no "I-sense" there is problem-free Consciousness. Why not meditate on it? I am not located in time and space. Insofar as they exist, they exist in me. The only true statement I can make is "I am omnipresent and eternal."

> Both the wise and ignorant regard the body as "I."
> The ignorant confine the "I" to the body.
> For the wise, the Self endlessly shines as the limitless Heart,
> which includes the body and the world. (17)

Both the wise and the ignorant experience pain. But the wise don't experience suffering as the ignorant do. Children resemble wise people because they don't experience psychological and intellectual pain. From every experience it is possible to come to a conclusion. When the sun arises, we conclude that it circled the earth. Knowing this fact does not change my experience, only my conclusion, even though my conclusion is not true. I experience hunger and conclude that I am the body. But when I think about it, I can't be the body, because the body is an object known to me. When I realize it is an object, I am free of it. Likewise with the mind. I know my thoughts. Obviously I am not them. Yet everyone says, "I think," which only goes to show the ubiquity and depth of Self-ignorance.

Without a subject, objects and instruments of experience, I can't have an experience. But I don't experience three things simultaneously when I experience. I only experience one thing at a time because there is only one me from which my experiencing instruments are non-separate. If reality was a conscious subject plus sentient and insentient objects, I still wouldn't experience duality, because experience is just Awareness plus the thought dominating the mind-stuff at the time. If thoughts come from anywhere, they can only come from me. So when I'm experiencing you, I'm experiencing me.

I don't see. I am Seeing.

The world exists for both the ignorant and the wise.
But only the ignorant see the world as real.
For the wise, the formless source of the seen
is the only reality. [18]

The one who is ignorant of the Self thinks the waking, dream and deep-sleep states are real, whereas the wise think the three states are unreal and the knower of them is real. Negation of the world is not negation of the experience of the world, only the reality of the world.

Inference and direct perception die with the death of the ego. An individual sees "the formless source" by inference, which is as valid a means of knowledge as direct perception, but someone who has dropped their sense of individuality "sees" the formless source as the formless source.

Questioning the relative merits of free will and fate is only for those who do not know their source.
Those who know the one for whom they pertain remain untouched by them. [19]

A Defect of Cause and Effect

Just as it is impossible to tell if birth creates *karma* or *karma* creates birth or a chicken creates an egg or an egg creates a chicken, it is impossible to determine if fate and free will are real, because they are mutually interdependent.

Understanding this fact is liberation because it shows that there is no Creation at all. There is no Creation because creation involves three factors, which are only possible because there are two factors, Awareness and matter. But there is only one non-dual source, which is immutable, which is me. How can an immutable substrate generate two things? Reality is one without a second. If there were two sources, duality would be a fact. But there is only one, so duality is purely imagination, *Maya*.

Therefore we can't blame God for our *karma*. We can only blame our ignorance of What we are. If you say suffering is a matter of chance, you run up against the fact that the Creation is a consciously designed matrix of laws. Finally, you can't blame Awareness either, because it is non-dual and impartial. Fate is just an individual's *karmic* account fructifying. If you are a dualist, you can only define freedom as bondage to God, since you will only be considered a devotee if you surrender your will to God's. But God doesn't have a will, because God is not an agent.

Although *karma yoga* is duality, a *karma yogi* is going for freedom from bondage, including bondage to God. Although a *karma yogi* takes the results of his actions as God's comment on the nature of his actions, he takes responsibility for results until he transcends the God-concept. He does actions in harmony with the cosmic order that mitigate unhelpful *karma* and generate helpful *karma*.

The free-will controversy is only for people who are ignorant of the cause of their "I-sense." When ignorance is known to be the cause, blame disappears and surrender to the process of Self-inquiry is inevitable.

Seeing Is Knowing Is Abiding

To see God apart from the seer is only a mental image,
since God is not separate from the seer.
To abide in the poise of the Self
is true vision of God. [20]

The *Upanishads* don't say if God is real or apparently real, because the meaning of words depends on your definition. If God is the Creator, then God won't be Existence/Awareness, because it is immutable. Nor is it an agent that can create. Even if it was a person, it is not incomplete, meaning it would be eternally self-satisfied, so the idea of creating objects of enjoyment is not present in it. So a seemingly independent principle must be responsible for the Creation, which Vedanta calls *Maya*, in which case God would be seemingly existent, meaning as good as non-existent. Vedanta is not an atheistic philosophy as some claim. To dismiss God, God has to exist in the first place, but if the world doesn't exist apart from the concept of it, the Creator is nothing but a thought in the mind of a person who doesn't know the nature of reality.

Ramana defines God as Existence/Awareness because, if there is an independent principle, it couldn't create without the presence of Awareness, in which case it would be a dependent principle, or *mithya*, seemingly dependent. Ramana calls a dependent God a mental image, meaning a purely conceptual entity. At the same time, he doesn't address the issue of creativity. So we can only conclude that there is no actual Creation, which means that an apparent Creation, like a dream, is as good as no Creation whatsoever.

I don't want to see God.

The scriptures declare, "see the Self," "see God."
But because it is one without a second, it cannot be seen.
See God by being swallowed by Him. (21)

I do not want to see God. Whatever vision I might have would only be a subjective experience, a light/love experience or an objective experience, seeing insentient God in a sunset, a panoramic vista or a stone. Seeing God in this way, you don't you realize you are only seeing yourself. No remote God created nature.

Ramana's definition of God is Existence shining as Awareness, which leaves no room for duality, because there is only Existence. So the only way is to let go of the notion that you are a separate experiencer. Allow yourself to be swallowed by Self-knowledge. The ego is rooted in the darkness of ignorance, which can only be "consumed" by the light of knowledge, not a particular experience. Seeing is simply non-conceptual knowing. It is the nature of all sentient beings.

God illumines the mind and shines within it, unseen.
How then can one know God through the mind?
Turning the mind inward and fixing it in Him

alone is to have His vision. [22]

Matter is insentient. Illumined by Existence shining as Awareness, sentient beings evolve. *Jivas* are extroverts, hypnotized by the thoughts arising in the mind, so they don't feel the silent Awareness that is illuming the mind. Ramana says Self-inquiry is fixing the mind on Awareness, which means ignoring the thoughts because they are not real, or "not-Self." Because they are not real, you should not identify with and follow them, as they only lead to more discrete experiences. And what does the meditator experience when the senses are withdrawn and the mind is turned inward? Silence. And what is this silence? It is Awareness reflecting in the pure portion of the mind-stuff. Is experiencing the silence experiencing God? No. Why? Because where there is duality, the experiencer has not been swallowed by the Self.

So what is experiencing the silence? Consciousness. What kind of experience is it? Witnessing experience (*sakshi bhava*), which is not experience as the "I-sense" experiences, because the witness is not modified in any way by what is experienced, which is to say it is free of experience.

How can I remove duality? By contemplating the non-dual teachings until the mind assimilates them. Assimilated Self-knowledge destroys the apparent experiencer, leaving only me, Awareness, shining alone.

Beautiful, intelligent Ignorance.

The body does not say I.
Only fools say they do not exist in deep sleep.
When the "I-sense" appears, the world arises.
Find out with keen intellect, whence this "I"? [23]

The "I-sense" or "I-notion" is a mysterious fictional mixture of Awareness and matter. The one non-dual entity appears as two by the grace of Ignorance. There is no third entity called "me."

Consciousness can't say "I am," because it has no organs. The body can't say "I am," because it is insentient. Only when Awareness illumines the mind does a third mysterious entity, a sentient being, endowed with the power to speak appears. No one should say they don't exist in sleep, because they can't wake or dream or sleep unless they exist. If you try to locate that sentient being, you cannot find it. It is only a "sense of self," not an actual Self.

37

How does the body arise? It evolves out of the three *gunas*, the permutations and combinations of which produce the multiplicity of names and forms available for experience. Prior to the appearance of matter, Existence/Awareness exists. Then Ignorance – *Maya*, the three *gunas* – appears as matter and sentient beings. Matter appears first as space, which divides and recombines to make the elements, after which *jivas* evolve.

Jivas begin as unicellular organisms and become increasingly complex. At first they are completely extroverted but over time the experiencing instrument bifurcates and part of their minds turn around; when they become self-reflective, they are called human beings. First humans think only about their relationship to the world, then they start thinking about their relationship with themselves. First they think they are their emotions and thoughts. A few eventually realize there is something beyond their minds, and because they are naturally curious, they begin to seek it. Then Awareness reveals itself to particularly *sattvic* Ramanas in every age, and the *Upanishads* appear. Contemplating them as taught by a qualified teacher destroys the belief that the "I-sense" is me.

> The body does not arise, because it is insentient. The Self does not arise.
> Within and between the body and the Self an insubstantial knot like "I" arises.
> It is called "I-sense," subtle body, ego and mind. [24]

The Reflection Teaching

Your face in a mirror has features of your face and features of the mirror. If the mirror shakes, your features appear to move, but they don't move, because the mirror is responsible for the movement. The face "borrows" the movement from the mirror. If the mind is active, it seems like you, Existence/Awareness, are moving. If the mirror is dirty, your face will look dirty. The I-notion is like the mirror, subject to change. When you look in the mirror, you think you are looking at yourself. But you can't see the Self, which is the Consciousness that is aware of the you that is looking. It never appears in the mirror.

Asking for it to appear is foolish, although people pray to God to "see" God. If you turn the mirror away from your face, the face disappears. Likewise, if you separate the material part of your Self from the witnessing part, the person disappears. It is like a mirage, only created by conditions. If it disappears, is it a real entity? People feel inauthentic because they take themselves to be the reflected self. The feeling is true because this insubstantial entity is a fake. The reflected self is variously called a thinker, a feeler, a doer, the mind, a person, me, *samsara*, etc. Miraculously it binds the Self to the not-Self until it is swallowed by the words of the teacher.

> Born of forms, rooted in forms,
> feeding on forms, ever changing its forms,
> itself formless, this ego-ghost
> takes to its heels on enquiry. [25]

The I-sense is borrowed from Existence shining as Awareness. Its survival is dependent on the properties and qualities of matter. This fraudulent person is never the same from moment to moment. A disturbed poseur, it dies in sleep but springs to life when the alarm goes off and the day's *karma* kicks in. Addicted to doing, it experiences joy and sorrow woven fine as the mental-material mirror vibrates and oscillates. Because its thoughts torment it and it is unable to control them, it thinks inquiry is just another useless mental activity.

Shifting your backpack.

> When the ego arises, your world arises.
> When it subsides, experiences subside.
> All experiences are just your I-sense changing.
> Tracking it is the way to victory over everything. [26]

Trying to change yourself or the world is like shifting your backpack from one shoulder to the other. It feels good for a while but eventually becomes a burden.

> The "I" does not arise in the real state.
> Investigating the source of "I" dissolves it.
> How else can one attain
> the supreme state of one's own Self? [27]

The ego is rooted in ignorance, the mud of *samsara*. Self-knowledge, produced by exposing the mind to Vedanta, destroys the belief that it is real, shifting your identity to the Self, and bliss becomes the dominant, permanent feature of your experience. There is no other way that a *jiva* can experience its natural state. The *Gita* says, "Once you 'go there' you never come back." If you do come back, it means that ignorance is still in control. The only way to get back to where you belong is to continue to contemplate the teachings. How does Vedanta destroy the ego? It proves the world is *mithya*, seemingly real. The snake disappears when the rope is revealed.

Sense pleasures suppress the I-sense, and the Self experiences reflected experiential bliss, which is non-separate from the bliss of the Self. Is moonlight not just reflected sunlight?

> With a keen intellect discover the real source of the ego
> by exploring within, regulating the breath, speech and mind
> as one would do to recover an object
> which has fallen into a deep well. (28)

For a qualified, purified person, Vedanta is a cakewalk. For an unqualified person, it is totally unappealing, because it involves disciplining the body, mind and intellect.

> To enquire silently and deeply as to the source
> of the mind, the "I" alone is Self-enquiry.
> Ideas like "I am that" or "I am not this"
> are but aids. (29)

Ignorance is the source of the mind and is hardwired into it. A one-off insight or even a mind-blowing epiphany will not dislodge it. Silence itself will not dispel ignorance, but the words of scripture – God's words – spoken by a qualified *mahatma* to a qualified inquirer produce *savikalpa samadhi*, silence with thought, assuming they share a common vocabulary. In this *samadhi*, it is possible to assimilate knowledge.

Self-inquiry is not asking or exploring on one's own without the benefit of a valid means of knowledge and a competent teacher, someone who has assimilated the knowledge from his or her teacher. It is not questioning. It is immediately seeing the truth of the revealing words as they appear in the mirror of Vedanta as unfolded by the teacher. Sitting in a quiet place or in the presence of someone who doesn't speak will not remove the "I-sense." Silence is cozy with ignorance. Only the light of truth will remove the darkness of ignorance. Truth needs to be heard. A mind focused in this way does not need to reflect on the teachings. There is nothing to remember. Knowledge washes away ignorance, and evaporates.

In this text, Ramana does not explain how this is done, so we need to revert to other *prakarana* texts which say that an unprepared mind cannot remove the ego, because it thinks it *is* an ego. It wants to add a particular experience of Existence/Consciousness that it thinks will justify its claim to egolessness. Egolessness simply means that "I am limitless Existence/Awareness" since It has no ego. Teaching is not for the ego, because the ego is inert, a conceptual entity. It is for the Self under the spell of ignorance. An unqualified ignorant Self does not accept the idea that it is the Self already and that ignorance is its problem. Ramana does not explain how to apply the mind. That it is required, however, is clear. Furthermore, it is little wonder that the modern Ramana cult eschews *Sat Darshanam*, because Ramana makes it clear that without the four "D"s – discrimination, dispassion, devotion and desire for Self-knowledge – the I-sense will remain mired in the quicksand of ignorance.

> The ego falls, crestfallen, when one enquires
> "Who am I?" and enters the Heart.
> Then, another I throbs unceasingly, by itself.
> It is not the ego, but the whole and complete Self itself. (30)

Inquiry converts the unknown to the known. The whole and complete Self has no room for attributes. Once the knowledge comes, one's actions become motiveless. "Enters" and "throbs" are metaphors.

> Who can understand the state of the one
> that has dissolved the ego and is abiding always as the Self?
> For him, the Self alone is. What is left to do? (31)

The negated ego becomes a vessel. Existence shines as Awareness through a purified subtle body blessing the world.

The scriptures assert "THAT YOU ARE."

> Without enquiring, reaching and abiding as the ever-shining Self,
> endless discussion about the Self is due to weakness of mind. (32)

It is difficult to separate the means from the end. Because Vedanta delivers so much joy, it is possible to settle for the joyful means. However, Vedanta is only another insentient object, a complete teaching that removes ignorance and removes itself.

The eye of wisdom sees itself.

Statements like "I do not know myself"
or "I know who I am" are a matter for laughter.
Are there two selves, the seer and the seen?
The experience of all is that the Self is one. [33]

The eyes can see any object but themselves, but Vedanta is unique among means of knowledge, because the seer and the seen are revealed to be identical.

Knowing as a process is necessary only when there is ignorance of something, but that I am a conscious being is so well known no one feels the need to inform us. Consequently there is no other way to know the Self but to know what "I am" means. But I may not know what it means to be "conscious being" in terms of the world in which my equipment exists. So Vedanta focuses on removing projected attributes from Awareness, i.e. the ideas associated with the five sheaths.

I am not slim or fat, hungry or thirsty, angry or sad, smart or stupid, liberated or bound. I am not white or black, Christian or Muslim, man or woman. No adjectives apply to me. I can only say I am. No quality defines me. I define and defy all qualities.

Instead of firmly abiding in the Heart in one's own true state,
those who quarrel about "real" and "unreal," "form" and "formless,"
"many" or "one" are indeed blind. [34]

We quarrel about the teachings because the false center of our experience has not been removed by the teaching. Turning your attention to the Self is abiding in the thought "I am Existence shining as Awareness." It is living in the Heart as the Heart, one's essence. I will never let ignorance convert me into an enlightened being.

Self-abidance alone is a miracle.
Other miracles like dreams only last till waking.
Can those firmly rooted in the Real
return to Ignorance? [35]

If you are identified as the Self, the mind becomes powerful and the subtle body glows with increasing radiance, which makes the *jiva* particularly attractive. Sometimes this phenomenon brings worldly success. After he realized the Self, Ramana left the temple in town and moved to a cave on the mountainside, but as his fame grew he was forced by the adulation to move even further up the mountain, because people were disturbing his meditation. Eventually, he surrendered to the will of *Isvara* and allowed the devotees to build an *ashram* at the foot of the mountain where he was accessible to the public.

As the *Bhakti Sutras* point out, Self-realized people whose abidance is not one hundred percent are "in danger of a fall." Worldly tendencies that have not been completely destroyed by Self-knowledge can extrovert the mind to such a degree that one's life becomes a misery in spite of what one knows. Ramana says that overcoming ignorance is the only worthwhile miracle. Worldly success is delusional.

> As long as we think the body is the Self,
> it is useful to claim "I am the Self" for realizing That.
> But when one rediscovers one is That,
> claiming it is as futile as a man repeating,
> "I am a human being, I am a human being." [36]

Until "I am Awareness" becomes a fact for me, I should apply it to my mind on a moment-to-moment basis, but once it becomes a fact, it is no longer required. Liberation is freedom from the doer/enjoyer claimant. A person who claims to be free, but continues to claim it, is either narcissistic or needy or both. Rather than appearing as a feather in the apparent *jiva's* cap, Self-realization should inspire embarrassment. How could I have missed such an obvious simple truth after seeking it for so long? To prevent the "I-sense" from rising up again, liberation should be viewed as a loss of ignorance, not a gain in knowledge. Self-actualized people are neither proud or humble. They are.

I am free when I know and free when I don't know.

> The idea of duality during practice and
> non-duality on realization are not true.
> The tenth man existed when he was lost
> and when he was found. [37]

43

Non-duality is not a time-bound state, event or experience. Temporary non-duality is a name that refers to unmanifest duality. A non-duality that comes when duality goes is duality. Non-duality is a fact. Duality is a belief based on sense perception. Events and experiences are momentary apparent truths, not actual facts. Fire is always hot, whether I know it or not. Sugar is always sweet. Knowledge is always good. I am never born. I never die. To understand these facts, discrete experiences are sometimes helpful, sometimes detrimental. When you are suffering and Vedanta says you are the Self, you start looking for it without realizing it is the one who is looking.

Vedanta reveals the unexamined logic of one's own experience.

> Identified as a doer, one reaps the fruits of his actions.
> If you enquire, "Who is the doer?"
> and enter the Heart, the doership will end.
> Triple *karma* is destroyed. This indeed is liberation. [38]

The Self can't do, because it has no mind or instruments of action. The ego can't do, because it is an inert material concept. When the Self is under the spell of ignorance, it identifies with the body-mind, which is in a perpetual state of activity owing to the presence of Awareness. Consequently it thinks it is a doer. Vedanta reveals the unexamined logic of one's own experience which proves that the Self isn't a doer.

"Heart" means the essence. Obviously you can't enter the essence, because the essence of something is that which can't be entered. For instance, sweetness is the essence of sugar. If something other than sweetness is added, it is no longer sugar. The essence of everything, sentient and insentient, is blissful Existence shining as Awareness. Nothing can be added to it or subtracted from it. It is a partless whole. So "enters the Heart" is a figure of speech. It is addressed to the Self that thinks it is a doer and means "try to eliminate the eliminator," a rhetorical statement because you cannot eliminate something that is as good a non-existent.

Cancel Culture

The practice of inquiry is removing objects. The body is an object. It need not be physically removed. It needs to be canceled. It is canceled when you realize that the perceiver of the body can't be the body. They never meet. There is always a gap between them. Likewise with the mind. The doer too needs to be canceled, but it is more difficult because doing is our most lovable thought.

Everything we do is calculated to turn the doer into an enjoyer because we don't know we are ever-full actionless Awareness, the nature of which is Bliss. If anything is to be eliminated, it will have to be done by a conscious being. The ego can't cancel itself, because it is inert. But if it could, it wouldn't, because it thinks it wouldn't be present to enjoy the fruit of canceling.

We enter the Heart when we cancel our individuality. We see that we are not a conscious being; we are Being shining as Awareness. We exist and we know, which is to say we shine. Try to cancel the one that exists and knows. When we realize that it is impossible, we have "entered the Heart," which is to say we now "abide as Awareness."

When the doer is canceled, the *karma* standing in one's account waiting to fructify, the *karma* fructifying now and *karma* that will fructify in the future is canceled. Because there is actually no past, present or future, *karma* is not real. It is a concept based on the idea that I am the mind-body entity, which is not real either.

Self-inquiry, Vedanta, is the process of entering, i.e. understanding, one's essence, which eliminates the "I-sense" by default.

> Thoughts of liberation appear only so long as one thinks one is bound.
> One attains the eternally liberated I by the enquiry
> "For whom is bondage?"
> Thereafter, how can thought of freedom and bondage arise? [39]

If freedom is defined as the removal of bondage, there is no freedom, because the Self was never bound. Bondage is a thought, and inert things have no power to bind. If there is no bondage, how can it be removed? Saying that Vedanta removes bondage is a figurative expression that means: when one is clear that one's ever-present ordinary Awareness is not associated with the body-mind-sense complex, one's identity as Awareness, which is free of suffering, is secure. Only the thought "I am attached to this or that" is the problem, because we know that the body is mortal. When we find out that the Self is Existence/Awareness, we see that it cannot be mortal, that it transcends change. But Vedanta needs to pretend that it removes bondage or no one will listen to the teachings. Once someone listens attentively, he or she will figure out that bondage is just an idea.

Some scholars say that after liberation form remains.

> Others say they don't remain. Yet others say sometimes
> they remain and sometimes not. The loss of the I-sense,
> which is the basis of these three concepts, alone is true liberation. (40)

From the world's point of view, forms remain. From the *jiva's* point of view, forms don't remain, because the particular "I-sense" disappears when the body dies. The generic "I-sense" shared by all humans remains until the reflection illuminating the mind no longer shines. If the Self was nothing, ignorance would not remain. But when you have an existent thing, ignorance comes along with it. Fortunately, ignorance can be canceled.

Essence of the Teaching

Identification with the "I-sense" is a poisonous snake, the cause of all problems. The only antidote is Self-inquiry. We project reality on it due to the poison of ignorance. It should be defanged by a keeping the mind innocent and exposed to the teachings of Vedanta.

Printed in the USA
CPSIA information can be obtained
at www.ICGtesting.com
LVHW011935050124
768156LV00001B/280